DISCOVER!

I0876248

EARTH AND SPACE SCIENCE

EARTH'S SURFACE

Beth Irving

Enslow PUBLISHING

Please visit our website, www.enslow.com. For a free color catalog of all our high-quality books, call toll free 1-800-398-2504 or fax 1-877-980-4454.

Cataloging-in-Publication Data
Names: Irving, Beth.
Title: Earth's surface / Beth Irving.
Description: Buffalo, NY : Enslow Publishing, 2027. | Series: Earth and space science | Includes glossary and index.
Identifiers: ISBN 9781978550261 (pbk.) | ISBN 9781978550278 (library bound) | ISBN 9781978550285 (ebook)
Subjects: LCSH: Earth (Planet)–Surface–Juvenile literature. | Landforms–Juvenile literature. | Earth (Planet)–Crust–Juvenile literature.
Classification: LCC QE511.I785 2027 | DDC 551.3–dc23

Published in 2027 by
Enslow Publishing
2544 Clinton Street
Buffalo, NY 14224

Designer: Claire Vanden Branden
Editor: Noah Riccardi

Photo Credits: Cover, p. 1 John Graybosch/Shutterstock.com; p. 5 Maxx-Studio/Shutterstock.com; p. 6 Elena Berd/Shutterstock.com; p. 7 Yvonnefollansbee22/Shutterstock.com; p. 9 Eleseus/Shutterstock.com; p. 10 anmbph/Shutterstock.com; p. 11 Ondrej Bucek/Shutterstock.com; p. 13 Natalia Bratslavsky/Shutterstock.com; p. 15 Tetyana Ohare/Shutterstock.com; p. 17 Janice Chen/Shutterstock.com; p. 19 Somchaij/Shutterstock.com; p. 21 b-hide the scene/Shutterstock.com.

Printed in China

CPSIA compliance information: Batch #QS27ENS: For further information contact Enslow Publishing, at 1-800-398-2504.

CONTENTS

BOLDFACE WORDS APPEAR IN THE GLOSSARY.

EARTH'S LANDFORMS

It's a lot of fun to **explore** Earth's **surface**. You can see many kinds of land when you're exploring. These are called landforms.

Earth has several **layers**. The layer we stand on is called the crust. Under the crust is a layer called the mantle. The mantle is solid and very hot. It's so hot that rocks can **melt**!

The melted rock can come out of the earth through volcanoes. A volcano is a tall landform with a hole on top. After the melted rock comes out, it cools to form new land. Cooled rock from volcanoes in the ocean can build up and form islands.

HIGH LANDFORMS

Earth's crust is made of many pieces. These pieces are always moving. They move very slowly. Mountains form when pieces of the crust push against each other.

Mountains are very high landforms. They stand much taller than the land around them. The tallest part of a mountain is called the peak.

A plateau is another high landform. It’s different from a mountain because it doesn’t have a peak. It has a flat top.

Plateaus are often close to mountains. The Altiplano in South America is a big plateau. It's close to the huge Andes mountains.

OUT ON THE PLAINS

Plains are flat landforms, too. But plains aren't high like plateaus. They're low landforms. The United States has the Great Plains. Many kinds of grasses grow there.

Plains are great for farming. There are many farms on the Great Plains. We use the wheat that farmers grow there to make bread.

RIVERS AND VALLEYS

Rivers flow over the land. They also shape the land. Rivers **erode** dirt and rock. They change the way that the land looks.

Some rivers create valleys. Valleys are low landforms. You can find them between mountains.

Other valleys are made by glaciers. A glacier is a huge piece of ice. Glaciers grow bigger as more snow falls on them.

Glaciers start to flow downhill when they get too heavy. They're like slow-moving rivers of ice. A moving glacier can cut through the ground. This makes a valley.

CANYONS CALLING

Canyons are a special kind of valley. You can find a canyon between two **cliffs**. Canyons are very deep landforms.

Rivers can also create canyons. In Arizona, you can see the Colorado River running through the Grand Canyon. Over a very long time, the river created the canyon.

EXPLORING LANDFORMS

There are so many landforms to see! They tell us a lot about Earth's history. By studying mountains and valleys, we can figure out how Earth used to look millions of years ago.

It's fun to visit landforms, too. What kinds of landforms would you like to explore?

GLOSSARY

cliffs: High, steep pieces of rock.

erode: To break down and carry away.

explore: To search something to find out more about it.

layers: Pieces that go over or under other pieces.

melt: To change from hard to soft using heat.

surface: The top part that can be seen.

FOR MORE INFORMATION

Books

Doeden, Matt. *34 Amazing Facts about Natural Wonders*. Minneapolis, MN: Lerner Publications, 2024.

Layton, Christine. *Wyoming*. Minneapolis, MN: Abdo Publishing, 2025.

Websites

Britannica Kids: Volcano
kids.britannica.com/kids/article/volcano/353902
Learn more about volcanoes at this site.

National Geographic Kids: Yellowstone
kids.nationalgeographic.com/nature/article/yellowstone
Learn about Yellowstone National Park, one of Earth's most amazing landscapes.

Publisher's note to educators and parents: Our editors have carefully reviewed these websites to ensure that they are suitable for students. Many websites change frequently, however, and we cannot guarantee that a site's future contents will continue to meet our high standards of quality and educational value. Be advised that students should be closely supervised whenever they access the internet.

INDEX